THE PENGUIN POETS

D 17

C. DAY LEWIS

Selected Poems

C. DAY LEWIS

PENGUIN BOOKS

HARMONDSWORTH · MIDDLESEX

First published by Penguin Books 1951

*Made and Printed in Great Britain
for Penguin Books Ltd
by Hunt, Barnard and Co Ltd*

CONTENTS

PREFACE

The publisher has asked me to write a preface for this volume of my selected poems. About the choice of them there is little to be said, except that they had to be taken in fairly equal proportions from my earlier books, published by the Hogarth Press, and my more recent ones, published by Jonathan Cape. The latter work is placed first in the present volume, followed by two narrative poems which appeared in the middle and late Thirties, with some of my earlier poems in the third section. To what extent this selection is 'representative', or might enable a reader to 'trace the poet's development', I cannot say. Looking back over my verse of the last twenty years, to make the selection, I was struck, as I have been before, by its lack of development – in the sense of one poetic phase emerging recognizably from the previous one and leading inevitably to the next: it would be all much tidier and more in accordance with critical specifications, were this not so. But my verse seems to me a series of fresh beginnings, rather than a continuous line. Change I *can* see: change, but I hope not decay. My later work, as far as I may judge, presents a good deal more variety both in subject matter and in verse forms, a more sensuous appeal, and a greater flexibility of line, than my earlier. This is partly, no doubt, because my interests have changed and my sympathies perhaps widened. At the same time, it is only fair to inform the reader that, in the view of some critics, my verse has deteriorated since the early 'school of social consciousness' days into an anti-social or at any rate a-social preoccupation with the past and with traditional forms.

Change of character there certainly has been. Not that poems are often the *immediate* product of such changes. What happens, as far as I can make out, is that I have some deep violent experience which, like an earthquake, throws up layers of my past that were inaccessible to me poetically till then. During the last war, for instance, I found myself able to use in verse for the first time images out of my own childhood. The new material thrown up, the new contours which life presents as a result of the seismic experience, may demand a new kind of poem. It is here that change of technique appears. If the poet is, as Yeats became, an original poet, this change will be largely an affair between his imagination and his new material. If, like myself, he is a writer still much open to the influence of other poets, he will often find that he has more or less consciously used some other poet to mediate between his material and his imagination. I myself have been technically influenced, and enabled to clarify my thoughts, by such diverse poets as Yeats, Wordsworth, Robert Frost, Vergil, Valéry, W. H. Auden, and Hardy. They suggested to me ways of saying what I had to say. Any given poem thus influenced is not necessarily secondhand: I think it possible that a reader with a sensitive ear, a dispassionate point of view, and a thorough knowledge of the poetry of Hardy, say, would find as much difference as similarity between a poem of mine, influenced by him, and one of Hardy's own.

But that is by the way. What is important is that the reader should become aware both of the uniqueness of a poem and of its family resemblances. To realise its uniqueness – the quality that makes it different from every other poem – he must respond to it directly, spontaneously, positively. To approach a new poem, armed with all the latest instruments of criticism, and ask these to tell us whether we ought to admire or dislike it, is none the less an imbecility for being rather common practice to-day. We must be able to enjoy before we can learn to discriminate. The chief value of criticism, for the ordinary reader, is to deepen his understanding of a poem which already appeals to him, by indicating its family likenesses – its affinities in style, thought and experience, with other poems; its place in the tradition. But tradition is not a museum: it is a two-way traffic. The major poets, who enlarge the tradition, not only open the way for a new poetry; their own work is illuminated, reflected back on, by the work of lesser poets they influence. So we must never think of 'modern poetry' as something in a vacuum, or something that started in 1900, or 1917, or 1930. Every good poem has grown out of the compost of all the poetry ever written, just as every original poet has been accused in his time, as poets are to-day, of obscurity, of breaking the rules and flouting the tradition. Modern poetry is every poem, whether written last year or five centuries ago, that has meaning for us still. In all ages there have been people narking about the incompetence and unintelligibility of the verse of their contemporaries, and other people acclaiming it as the highest peak of poetic achievement, and yet other people to tell each poet exactly how he ought to be writing and conducting his life. These nuisances may do a certain amount of damage temporarily. But time sorts it all out. And in the meantime each poet must go on writing as best he may, learning from his own mistakes, learning to stop worrying about his stature, his rank in the hierarchy (for 'there is no competition'), and to become ever more fully absorbed by the immediate task.

A poem, Robert Frost has said, 'begins in delight and ends in wisdom'. This is true, in a way, for the writer also. Poetry is a vocation, a habit, and a search for truth. We begin, young, with no equipment but a love for words and a special kind of temperament. We go on writing verse, if we do go on, because it has become a habit to play with words and to rely on them for the orientation of our interests. As we accumulate experience, we begin to perceive, sooner or later, that every poem is an attempt to compose our memories and to interpret this experience to our own satisfaction. We write in order to understand, not in order to be understood; though, the more successfully a poem has interpreted to its writer the meaning of his own experience, the more widely will it be 'understood' in the long run. The reader's progress is something similar. As a child he will have delighted in

words and rhythms for their own sake. In adolescence, and perhaps for some years later, if he reads poetry at all, he is looking
chiefly for a personal relevance: he wants the poem which will
accord with his own kind of fantasies about life or support his
fragmentary knowledge of it. It is only when we have done much
and suffered much that we are able at all surely to distinguish the
poetry in which sensuous and moral truth lie deepest; and by
then, too often, our literary sympathies have hardened, so that
we are prevented by its unfamiliar idiom from recognizing such
truth in new poetry when we see it. Concerning poetic truth –
that is, the re-ordering, re-creating and interpreting of human
experience through poetry – both poet and reader have to make
an act of faith. Each must believe that life holds certain kinds of
truth which can best, or only, be conveyed through the medium
of art, and that poetry has not been superseded in this function
by any other art. It is a difficult faith to-day. Yet it is vindicated
every time a poem, receiving the assent of heart and mind
together, makes us feel, if only for an hour, at one with life and
whole in ourselves.

It may be that such generalizations are out of place in a preface. I do not want the reader to think that absolute laws can be
laid down for the writing or the reading of poetry. Perhaps I
should, instead, have been taking him on a conducted tour of the
poems he can find in my own books, pointing out their beauties
and defects? I could show him where emotion, applied too raw,
has eaten holes in the fabric of a poem, and where it has been more
successfully depersonalized: where, through lack of patience, a
poem has taken a wrong turning and ended up in a blind alley; or
the very place where some apparently adventitious thing – the
need for a certain rhyme or cadence – gave me a line which
altered in the right direction a poem's whole course. I could
point out how, during my so-called 'political' period, most of my
poems were in fact about love or death: how, contrary to received

opinion about modern verse, nearly all my poems 'rhyme and scan'; and how, contrary to the preconceived opinions of some, they are not always less experimental in nature when they are more traditional in idiom: how an over-enthusiastic, often perfunctory use of 'modern' imagery is gradually replaced by a more personal yet wider field of images: how certain characteristics keep cropping up throughout my work – hero-worship, fear, compassion, the divided mind, a prevailing sense of the transience of things: and how, whatever its apparent focus of the moment – politics, the birth of a child, love for a woman, youthful memories, the apprehension or impact of war – however much its style is altered from time to time by the demands of some new experience or ruling passion, there runs through it all, an unbroken thread, the search for personal identity, the poet's relentless compulsion to know himself.

But it is best that the reader should discover such points for himself. Many of them he would find equally applicable to any other living poet. Besides, the poet is not the best expositor of his own work; for, if there is one thing which surpasses his ardour of concentration in writing a poem, it is the extreme sense of detachment he feels when it has been written. This is not the kind of detachment which is proper in a critic: it is that of the maker who, knowing that 'every attempt is a wholly new start and a different kind of failure', must cut himself free from each failure in order to make the next attempt.

C. DAY LEWIS

NOTE

OF the poems here reprinted, 'The Innocent', 'O Dreams, O Destinations', 'Cornet Solo', 'The Poet', 'The Rebuke', 'Jig', 'Hornpipe', 'The Album', and 'Departure in the Dark' were published in *Word Over All* (Cape, 1943); 'Passage from Childhood', 'Sex-Crime', and 'The Nabara' in *Overtures to Death* (Cape, 1938); the remaining poems of the first section (Lyrical and Reflective Poems 1937-47) in *Poems* 1943-7 (Cape, 1948); 'Flight to Australia' and all those in Section III (Lyrical and Reflective Poems 1929-36) in *Collected Poems* 1929-36 (Hogarth Press, 1948). The author thanks the Hogarth Press and Jonathan Cape Ltd for allowing them to be included in this selection.

I

Lyrical and Reflective Poems
1937–47

THE INNOCENT

A FORWARD child, a sullen boy,
My living image in the pool,
The glass that made me look a fool –
He was my judgement and my joy.

The bells that chimed above the lake,
The swans asleep in evening's eye,
Bright transfers pressed on memory
From him their gloss and anguish take.

When I was desolate, he came
A wizard way to charm my toys:
But when he heard a stranger's voice
He broke the toys, I bore the shame.

I built a house of crystal tears
Amid the myrtles for my friend:
He said, no man has ever feigned
Or kept the lustre of my years.

Later, a girl and I descried
His shadow on the fern-flecked hill,
His double near our bed: and still
The more I lived, the more he died.

Now a revenant slips between
The fine-meshed minutes of the clock
To weep the time we lost and mock
All that my desperate ditties mean.

PASSAGE FROM CHILDHOOD

His earliest memory, the mood
Fingered and frail as maidenhair,
Was this – a china cup somewhere
In a green, deep wood.
He lives to find again somewhere
That wood, that homely cup; to taste all
Its chill, imagined dews; to dare
The dangerous crystal.

Who can say what misfeatured elf
First led him into that lifelong
Passage of mirrors where, so young,
He saw himself
Balanced as Blondin, more headstrong
Than baby Hercules, rare as a one-
Cent British Guiana, above the wrong
And common run?

He knew the secrecy of squirrels,
The foolish doves' antiphony,
And what wrens fear. He was gun-shy,
Hating all quarrels.
Life was a hostile land to spy,
Full of questions he dared not ask
Lest the answer in mockery,
Or worse, unmask.

Quick to injustice, quick he grew
This hermit and contorted shell.
Self-pity like a thin rain fell,
Fouling the view:
Then tree-trunks seemed wet roots of hell,
Wren or catkin might turn vicious,
The dandelion clock could tell
Nothing auspicious.

No exile has ever looked so glum
With the pines fretful overhead,
Yet he felt at home in the gothic glade –
More than at home.
You will forgive him that he played
Bumble-puppy on the small mossed lawn
All by himself for hours, afraid
Of being born.

Lying awake one night, he saw
Eternity stretched like a howl of pain:

He was tiny and terrible, a new pin
On a glacier's floor.
Very few they are who have lain
With eternity and lived to tell it:
There's a secret process in his brain
And he cannot sell it.

Now, beyond reach of sense or reason,
His life walks in a glacial sleep
For ever, since he drank that cup
And found it poison.
He's one more ghost, engaged to keep
Eternity's long hours and mewed
Up in live flesh with no escape
From solitude.

O DREAMS, O DESTINATIONS

I

FOR infants time is like a humming shell
Heard between sleep and sleep, wherein the shores
Foam-fringed, wind-fluted of the strange earth dwell
And the sea's cavernous hunger faintly roars.

It is the humming pole of summer lanes
Whose sound quivers like heat-haze endlessly
Over the corn, over the poppied plains –
An emanation from the earth or sky.
Faintly they hear, through the womb's lingering haze,
A rumour of that sea to which they are born:
They hear the ringing pole of summer days,
But need not know what hungers for the corn.
They are the lisping rushes in a stream –
Grace-notes of a profound, legato dream.

2

Children look down upon the morning-grey
Tissue of mist that veils a valley's lap;
Their fingers itch to tear it and unwrap
The flags, the roundabouts, the gala day.
They watch the spring rise inexhaustibly –
A breathing thread out of the eddied sand,
Sufficient to their day: but half their mind
Is on the sailed and glittering estuary.
Fondly we wish their mist might never break,
Knowing it hides so much that best were hidden:
We'd chain them by the spring, lest it should broaden
For them into a quicksand and a wreck.
But they slip through our fingers like the source,
Like mist, like time that has flagged out their course.

That was the fatal move, the ruination
Of innocence so innocently begun,
When in the lawless orchard of creation
The child left this fruit for that rosier one.
Reaching towards the far thing, we begin it;
Looking beyond, or backward, more and more
We grow unfaithful to the unique minute
Till, from neglect, its features stale and blur.
Fish, bird or beast was never thus unfaithful –
Man only casts the image of his joys
Beyond his senses' reach; and by this fateful
Act, he confirms the ambiguous power of choice.
Innocence made that first choice. It is she
Who weeps, a child chained to the outraged tree.

4

Our youthtime passes down a colonnade
Shafted with alternating light and shade.
All's dark or dazzle there. Half in a dream
Rapturously we move, yet half afraid
Never to wake. That diamond-point, extreme
Brilliance engraved on us a classic theme:
The shaft of darkness had its lustre too,
Rising where earth's concentric mysteries gleam.
Oh youth-charmed hours, that made an avenue
Of fountains playing us on to love's full view,

A cypress walk to some romantic grave –
Waking, how false in outline and in hue
We find the dreams that flickered on our cave:
Only your fire, which cast them, still seems true.

5

All that time there was thunder in the air:
Our nerves branched and flickered with summer
        lightning.
The taut crab-apple, the pampas quivering, the glare
On the roses seemed irrelevant, or a heightening
At most of the sealed-up hour wherein we awaited
What? – some explosive oracle to abash
The platitudes on the lawn? heaven's delegated
Angel – the golden rod, our burning bush?
No storm broke. Yet in retrospect the rose
Mounting vermilion, fading, glowing again
Like a fire's heart, that breathless inspiration
Of pampas grass, crab-tree's attentive pose
Never were so divinely charged as then –
The veiled Word's flesh, a near annunciation.

6

Symbols of gross experience! – our grief
Flowed, like a sacred river, underground:
Desire bred fierce abstractions on the mind,
Then like an eagle soared beyond belief.

Often we tried our breast against the thorn,
Our paces on the turf: whither we flew,
Why we should agonize, we hardly knew --
Nor what ached in us, asking to be born.
Ennui of youth! – thin air above the clouds,
Vain divination of the sunless stream
Mirror that impotence, till we redeem
Our birthright, and the shadowplay concludes.
Ah, not in dreams, but when our souls engage
With the common mesh and moil, we come of age.

7

Older, we build a road where once our active
Heat threw up mountains and the deep dales veined:
We're glad to gain the limited objective,
Knowing the war we fight in has no end.
The road must needs follow each contour moulded
By that fire in its losing fight with earth:
We march over our past, we may behold it
Dreaming a slave's dream on our bivouac hearth.
Lost the archaic dawn wherein we started,
The appetite for wholeness: now we prize
Half-loaves, half-truths – enough for the half-hearted,
The gleam snatched from corruption satisfies.
Dead youth, forgive us if, all but defeated,
We raise a trophy where your honour lies.

8

But look, the old illusion still returns,
Walking a field-path where the succory burns
Like summer's eye, blue lustre-drops of noon,
And the heart follows it and freshly yearns:
Yearns to the sighing distances beyond
Each height of happiness, the vista drowned
In gold-dust haze, and dreams itself immune
From change and night to which all else is bound.
Love, we have caught perfection for a day
As succory holds a gem of halcyon ray:
Summer burns out, its flower will tarnish soon –
Deathless illusion, that could so relay
The truth of flesh and spirit, sun and clay
Singing for once together all in tune!

9

To travel like a bird, lightly to view
Deserts where stone gods founder in the sand,
Ocean embraced in a white sleep with land;
To escape time, always to start anew.
To settle like a bird, make one devoted
Gesture of permanence upon the spray
Of shaken stars and autumns; in a bay
Beyond the crestfallen surges to have floated.

Each is our wish. Alas, the bird flies blind,
Hooded by a dark sense of destination:
Her weight on the glass calm leaves no impression,
Her home is soon a basketful of wind.
Travellers, we're fabric of the road we go;
We settle, but like feathers on time's flow.

CORNET SOLO

Thirty years ago lying awake,
Lying awake
In London at night when childhood barred me
From livelier pastimes, I'd hear a street-band break
Into old favourites – 'The Ash Grove', 'Killarney'
Or 'Angels Guard Thee'.

That was the music for such an hour –
A deciduous hour
Of leaf-wan drizzle, of solitude
And gaslight bronzing the gloom like an autumn
    flower –
The time and music for a boy imbrued
With the pensive mood.

I could have lain for hours together,
Sweet hours together,

Listening to the cornet's cry
Down wet streets gleaming like patent leather
Where beauties jaunted in cabs to their revelry,
Jewelled and spry.

Plaintive its melody rose or waned
Like an autumn wind
Blowing the rain on beds of aster,
On man's last bed: mournful and proud it complained
As a woman who dreams of the charms that graced her,
In young days graced her.

Strange how those yearning airs could sweeten
And still enlighten
The hours when solitude gave me her breast.
Strange they could tell a mere child how hearts may
        beat in
The self-same tune for the once-possessed
And the unpossessed.

Last night, when I heard a cornet's strain,
It seemed a refrain
Wafted from thirty years back – so remote an
Echo it bore: but I felt again
The prophetic mood of a child, too long forgotten,
Too lightly forgotten.

THE POET

For me there is no dismay
Though ills enough impend.
I have learned to count each day
Minute by breathing minute –
Birds that lightly begin it,
Shadows muting its end –
As lovers count for luck
Their own heart-beats and believe
In the forest of time they pluck
Eternity's single leaf.

Tonight the moon's at the full.
Full moon's the time for murder.
But I look to the clouds that hide her –
The bay below me is dull,
An unreflecting glass –
And chafe for the clouds to pass,
And wish she suddenly might
Blaze down at me so I shiver
Into a twelve-branched river
Of visionary light.

For now imagination,
My royal, impulsive swan,
With raking flight – I can see her –
Comes down as it were upon
A lake in whirled snow-floss
And flurry of spray like a skier
Checking. Again I feel
The wounded waters heal.
Never before did she cross
My heart with such exaltation.

Oh, on this striding edge,
This hare-bell height of calm
Where intuitions swarm
Like nesting gulls and knowledge
Is free as the winds that blow,
A little while sustain me,
Love, till my answer is heard!
Oblivion roars below,
Death's cordon narrows: but vainly,
If I've slipped the carrier word.

Dying, any man may
Feel wisdom harmonious, fateful
At the tip of his dry tongue.
All I have felt or sung
Seems now but the moon's fitful
Sleep on a clouded bay,

Swan's maiden flight, or the climb
To a tremulous, hare-bell crest.
Love, tear the song from my breast!
Short, short is the time.

THE REBUKE

Down in the lost and April days
What lies we told, what lies we told!
Nakedness seemed the one disgrace,
And there'd be time enough to praise
The truth when we were old.

The irresponsible poets sung
What came into their head:
Time to pick and choose among
The bold profusions of our tongue
When we were dead, when we were dead.

Oh wild the words we uttered then
In woman's ear, in woman's ear,
Believing all we promised when
Each kiss created earth again
And every far was near.

Little we guessed, who spoke the word
Of hope and freedom high
Spontaneously as wind or bird
To crowds like cornfields still or stirred,
It was a lie, a heart-felt lie.

Now the years advance into
A calmer stream, a colder stream,
We doubt the flame that once we knew,
Heroic words sound all untrue
As love-lies in a dream.

Yet fools are the old who won't be taught
Modesty by their youth:
That pandemonium of the heart,
That sensual arrogance did impart
A kind of truth, a kindling truth.

Where are the sparks at random sown,
The spendthrift fire, the holy fire?
Who cares a damn for truth that's grown
Exhausted haggling for its own
And speaks without desire?

JIG

THAT winter love spoke and we raised no objection, at
Easter 'twas daisies all light and affectionate,
June sent us crazy for natural selection – not
Four traction-engines could tear us apart.
Autumn then coloured the map of our land,
Oaks shuddered and apples came ripe to the hand,
In the gap of the hills we played happily, happily,
Even the moon couldn't tell us apart.

Grave winter drew near and said, 'This will not do at all –
If you continue, I fear you will rue it all.'
So at the New Year we vowed to eschew it
Although we both knew it would break our heart.
But spring made hay of our good resolutions –
Lovers, you may be as wise as Confucians,
Yet once love betrays you he plays you and plays you
Like fishes for ever, so take it to heart.

HORNPIPE

Now the peak of summer's past, the sky is overcast
And the love we swore would last for an age seems deceit:
Paler is the guelder since the day we first beheld her
In blush beside the elder drifting sweet, drifting sweet.

Oh quickly they fade – the sunny esplanade,
Speed-boats, wooden spades, and the dunes where we've
    lain:
Others will be lying amid the sea-pinks sighing
For love to be undying, and they'll sigh in vain.

It's hurrah for each night we have spent our love so
    lightly
And never dreamed there might be no more to spend at
    all.
It's goodbye to every lover who thinks he'll live in
    clover
All his life, for noon is over soon and night-dews fall.

If I could keep you there with the berries in your hair
And your lacy fingers fair as the may, sweet may,
I'd have no heart to do it, for to stay love is to rue it
And the harder we pursue it, the faster it's away.

THE ALBUM

I SEE you, a child
In a garden sheltered for buds and playtime,
Listening as if beguiled
By a fancy beyond your years and the flowering
      maytime.
The print is faded: soon there will be
No trace of that pose enthralling,
Nor visible echo of my voice distantly calling
'Wait! Wait for me!'

Then I turn the page
To a girl who stands like a questioning iris
By the waterside, at an age
That asks every mirror to tell what the heart's desire is.
The answer she finds in that oracle stream
Only time could affirm or disprove,
Yet I wish I was there to venture a warning, 'Love
Is not what you dream.'

Next you appear
As if garlands of wild felicity crowned you –
Courted, caressed, you wear
Like immortelles the lovers and friends around you.
'They will not last you, rain or shine,

They are but straws and shadows,'
I cry: 'Give not to those charming desperadoes
What was made to be mine.'

One picture is missing –
The last. It would show me a tree stripped bare
By intemperate gales, her amazing
Noonday of blossom spoilt which promised so fair.
Yet, scanning those scenes at your heyday taken,
I tremble, as one who must view
In the crystal a doom he could never deflect – yes, I too
Am fruitlessly shaken.

I close the book;
But the past slides out of its leaves to haunt me
And it seems, wherever I look,
Phantoms of irreclaimable happiness taunt me.
Then I see her, petalled in new-blown hours,
Beside me – 'All you love most there
Has blossomed again,' she murmurs, 'all that you missed
    there
Has grown to be yours '

IS IT FAR TO GO?

Is it far to go?
  A step – no further.
Is it hard to go?
  Ask the melting snow,
  The eddying feather.

What can I take there?
  Not a hank, not a hair.
What shall I leave behind?
  Ask the hastening wind,
  The fainting star.

Shall I be gone long?
  For ever and a day.
To whom there belong?
  Ask the stone to say,
  Ask my song.

Who will say farewell?
  The beating bell.
Will anyone miss me?
  That I dare not tell –
  Quick, Rose, and kiss me.

THE WOMAN ALONE

I

Take any place – this garden plot will do
Where he with mower, scythe or hook goes out
To fight the grass and lay a growing fever,
Volcanic for another, dead to me;
Meek is the ghost, a banked furnace the man.

Take any time – this autumn day will serve,
Ripe with grassed fruit, raw with departing wings,
When I, whom in my youth the season tempted
To oceanic amplitudes, bend down
And pick a rotting apple from the grass.

From every here and now a thread leads back
Through faithless seasons and devouring seas:
New blooms, dead leaves bury it not, nor combers
Break it – my life line and my clue: the same
That brought him safe out of a labyrinth.

So I, the consort of an absent mind,
The emerald lost in a green waste of time,
The castaway for whom all space is island –

To follow, find, escape, this thread in hand,
Warp myself out upon the swelling past.

2

Take any joy – the thread leads always on
To here and now: snow, silence, vertigo;
His frozen face; a woman who bewails not
Only because she fears one echoing word
May bring the avalanche about her ears.

Take any joy that was – here it remains,
Corruptless, irrecoverable, cold
As a dead smile, beneath the cruel glacier
That moved upon our kisses, lambs and leaves,
Stilled them, but will not let their forms dissolve.

O tomb transparent of my waxen joys!
O lifelike dead under the skin of ice!
O frozen face of love where my one treasure
Is locked, and the key lost! May I not share
Even the bare oblivion of your fate?

But dare I throw the past into one fire,
One burning cry to break the silence, break
The cataleptic snows, the dream of falling?
Last night I thought he stood beside my bed
And said, 'Wake up! You were dreaming. I am here.'

3

Take any grief – the maggot at the nerve,
The words that bore the skull like waterdrops,
The castaway's upon the foam-racked island,
The lurching figures of a mind's eclipse –
I have felt each and all as love decayed.

Yet every grief revives a fainting love.
They are love's children too; I live again
In them; my breast yearns to their innocent cruelty.
If only tears can float a stranded heart,
If only sighs can move it, I will grieve.

The pleasured nerve, the small-talk in the night,
The voyaging when isles were daisy-chains,
The dance of mere routine – if I could reach them
Again through this sick labyrinth of grief,
I would rejoice in it, to reach them so.

Alas, hull-down upon hope's ashen verge
Hastens the vessel that our joined hands launched,
Stretching my heart-strings out beyond endurance.
Ah, will they never snap? Can I not climb
The signal hill, and wave, and *mean* goodbye?

SEX-CRIME

FOR one, the sudden fantastic grimace
Above, the red clown's-grin ripping the chalk sad sky,
Hailstones hatched out of midsummer, a face
Blanched with love's vile reversal.

                          The spirit died
First – such blank amazement took away its breath,
And let the body cry
Through the short scuffle and infamy of death.
For the other, who knows what nice proportion of
      loathing
And lust conjured the deep devil, created
That chance of incandescence? Figures here prove
      nothing.
One step took him through the roaring waterfall
That closed like a bead-curtain, left him alone with the
      writhing
Of what he loved or hated.
His hands leapt out: they took vengeance for all
Denials and soft answers. There was one who said
Long since, 'rough play will end in tears'. There was
      Cain
In the picture-book. Forgotten. Here is one dead,
And one could never be whole again.

                         The news
Broke a Sunday inertia; ring after ring
Across that smug mirror went echoing
And fainting out to the dim margins of incredulity.
A few raw souls accuse
Themselves of this felony and find not guilty –
Acquitted on a mere alibi or technical point.
Most see it as an island eruption, viewed
From the safe continent; not dreaming the same fire
    pent
Within their clay that warps
The night with fluent alarm, their own wrath spewed
Through the red craters of that undistinguished corpse.
All that has reached them is the seismic thrill:
The ornaments vibrate on the shelf; then they are still.
Snugly we settle down
Into our velvet and legitimate bed,
While news-sheets are yet falling all over the town
Like a white ash. Falling on one dead
And one can never be whole again.

                         You watch him
Pulpited in the dock, preaching repentance
While the two professionals in fancy dress
Manoeuvre formally to score off him or catch him.
But grief has her conventions –
The opaque mask of misery will confess
Nothing, nor plead moving extenuations.

But you who crowd the court-room, will you never be
    called
To witness for the defence?

                          Accomplices,
All of you, now – though now is still too late –
Bring on the missing evidence! Reveal the coiled
Venom, the curse that needs
Only a touch to be articulate.
You, Judge, strip off! Show us the abscess boiling
Beneath your scarlet. Oh point, someone, to where it
    spreads
On every hand – the red, collusive stain . . .
All too well you have done your work: for one is dead,
And the other will not be whole again.

THE NEUROTIC

THE spring came round, and still he was not dead.
Skin of the earth deliciously powdered
With buttercups and daisies – oh, Proserpina
Refreshed by sleep, wild-cherry-garlanded
And laughing in the sallies of the willow-wren!
With lambs and lilies spring came round again.

Who would suppose, seeing him walk the meadows,
He walks a treadmill there, grinding himself
To powder, dust to greyer dust, or treads
An invisible causeway lipped by chuckling shadows?

Take his arm if you like, you'll not come near him.
His mouth is an ill-stitched wound opening: hear him.

'I will not lift mine eyes unto the hills
For there white lambs nuzzle and creep like maggots.
I will not breathe the lilies of the valley
For through their scent a chambered corpse exhales.
If a petal floats to earth, I am oppressed.
The grassblades twist, twist deep in my breast.'

The night came on, and he was still alive.
Lighted tanks of streets a-swarm with denizens
Darting to trysts, sauntering to parties.
How all the heart-fires twinkle! Yes, they thrive
In the large illusion of freedom, in love's net
Where even the murderer can act and the judge regret.

This man who turns a phrase and twiddles a glass
Seems far from that pale muttering magician
Pent in a vicious circle of dilemmas.
But could you lift his blue, thick gaze and pass
Behind, you would walk a stage where endlessly
Phantoms rehearse unactable tragedy.

'In free air captive, in full day benighted,
I am as one for ever out of his element
Transparently enwombed, who from a bathysphere
Observes, wistful, amazed, but more affrighted,

Gay fluent forms of life weaving around,
And dares not break the bubble and be drowned.'

His doomsdays crawled like lava, till at length
All impulse clogged, the last green lung consumed,
Each onward step required the sweat of nightmare,
Each human act a superhuman strength . . .
And the guillemot, clotted with oil, droops her head.
And the mouse between the elastic paws shams dead.

Death mask of a genius unborn:
Tragic prince of a rejected play:
Soul of suffering that bequeathed no myth:
A dark tower and a never-sounded horn. –
Call him what we will, words cannot ennoble
This Atlas who fell down under a bubble.

THE DOUBLE VISION

THE river this November afternoon
Rests in an equipoise of sun and cloud:
A glooming light, a gleaming darkness shroud
Its passage. All seems tranquil, all in tune.

Image and real are joined like Siamese twins:
Their doubles draw the willows, a brown mare
Drinks her reflection. There's no margin where
Substance leaves off, the illusory begins.

You and I by the river contemplate
Our ideal selves, glossed here, crystal-divined:
We yearn to them, knowing one sigh of wind
Will rub these precious figures from the slate.

It is not of their transience I'm afraid,
But thinking how most human loves protract
Themselves to unreality – the fact
Drained of its virtue by the image it made.

O double vision of the autumnal stream,
Teach me to bear love's fusion or diffusion!
O gems of purest water, pure illusion,
Answer my rays and cluster to a theme!

THE SITTING

(for Laurence Gowing)

So like a god I sit here,
One of those stone dreamers quarried from solitude,
A genius – if ever there was one – of the place:
The mountain's only child, lips aloof as a snow-line,
Forearms impassive along the cloud-base of aeons,
Eyes heavy on distance –
Graven eyes that flinch not, flash not, if eagles
Clap their wings in my face.

With hieratic gestures
He the suppliant, priest, interpreter, subtly
Wooing my virtue, officiates by the throne.
I know the curious hands are shaping, reshaping the
     image
Of what is only an image of things impalpable.
I feel how the eyes strain
To catch a truth behind the oracular presence –
Eyes that augur through stone.

And the god asks, 'What have I for you
But the lichenous shadow of thought veiling my temple,
The runnels a million time-drops have chased on my
     cheek?'
And the man replies, 'I will show you the creed of your
     bone, I'll draw you
The shape of solitude to which you were born.'
And the god cries, 'I am meek,
Brushed by an eagle's wing; and a voice bids me
Speak. But I cannot speak.'

The god thinks, Let him project, if
He must, his passionate shapings on my stone heart,
Wrestle over my body with his sprite,
Through these blind eyes imagine a skin-deep world in
     perspective:
Let him make, if he will, the crypt of my holy mountain
His own: let even the light

That bathes my temple become as it were an active
Property of his sight.

O man, O innocent artist
Who paint me with green of your fields, with amber or
     yellow
Of love's hair, red of the heart's blood, eyebright blue,
Conjuring forms and rainbows out of an empty mist –
Your hand is upon me, as even now you follow
Up the immortal clue
Threading my veins of emerald, topaz, amethyst,
And know not it ends in you.

DEPARTURE IN THE DARK

Nothing so sharply reminds a man he is mortal
As leaving a place
In a winter morning's dark, the air on his face
Unkind as the touch of sweating metal:
Simple goodbyes to children or friends become
A felon's numb
Farewell, and love that was a warm, a meeting place –
Love is the suicide's grave under the nettles.

Gloomed and clemmed as if by an imminent ice-age
Lies the dear world
Of your street-strolling, field-faring. The senses, curled
At the dead end of a shrinking passage,

Care not if close the inveterate hunters creep,
And memories sleep
Like mammoths in lost caves. Drear, extinct is the
       world,
And has no voice for consolation or presage.

There is always something at such times of the passover,
When the dazed heart
Beats for it knows not what, whether you part
From home or prison, acquaintance or lover –
Something wrong with the time-table, something
       unreal
In the scrambled meal
And the bag ready packed by the door, as though the
       heart
Has gone ahead, or is staying here for ever.

No doubt for the Israelites that early morning
It was hard to be sure
If home were prison or prison home: the desire
Going forth meets the desire returning.
This land, that had cut their pride down to the bone
Was now their own
By ancient deeds of sorrow. Beyond, there was nothing
       sure
But a desert of freedom to quench their fugitive
       yearnings.

At this blind hour the heart is informed of nature's
Ruling that man
Should be nowhere a more tenacious settler than
Among wry thorns and ruins, yet nurture
A seed of discontent in his ripest ease.
There's a kind of release
And a kind of torment in every goodbye for every man –
And will be, even to the last of his dark departures.

THE UNWANTED

O N a day when the breath of roses
   Plumpened a swooning breeze
And all the silken combes of summer
   Opened wide their knees,
Between two sighs they planted one –
A willed one, a wanted one –
And he will be the sign, they said, of our felicities.

Eager the loins he sprang from,
   Happy the sheltering heart:
Seldom had the seed of man
   So charmed, so clear a start.
And he was born as frail a one,
As ailing, freakish, pale a one
As ever the wry planets knotted their beams to thwart.

Sun locked up for winter;
  Earth an empty rind:
Two strangers harshly flung together
  As by a flail of wind.
Oh was it not a furtive thing,
  A loveless, damned, abortive thing –
This flurry of the groaning dust, and what it left
    behind!

Sure, from such warped beginnings
  Nothing debonair
Can come? But neither shame nor panic,
  Drugs nor sharp despair
Could uproot that untoward thing,
  That all too fierce and froward thing:
Willy-nilly born it was, divinely formed and fair.

STATUETTE: LATE MINOAN

GIRL of the musing mouth,
The mild archaic air,
For whom do you subtly smile?
Yield to what power or prayer
Breasts vernally bare?

I seem to be peering at you
Through the wrong end of time
That shrinks to a bright, far image –
Great Mother of earth's prime –
A stature sublime.

So many golden ages
Of sunshine steeped your clay,
So dear did the maker cherish
In you life's fostering ray,
That you warm us today.

Goddess or girl, you are earth.
The smile, the offered breast –
They were the dream of one
Thirsting as I for rest,
As I, unblest.

EMILY BRONTË

A LL is the same still. Earth and heaven locked in
A wrestling dream the seasons cannot break:
Shrill the wind tormenting my obdurate thorn trees,
Moss-rose and stone-chat silent in its wake.
Time has not altered here the rhythms I was rocked in,
Creation's throb and ache.

All is yet the same, for mine was a country
Stoic, unregenerate, beyond the power
Of man to mollify or God to disburden –
An ingrown landscape none might long endure
But one who could meet with a passion wilder-wintry
The scalding breath of the moor.

All is yet the same as when I roved the heather
Chained to a demon through the shrieking night,
Took him by the throat while he flailed my sibylline
Assenting breast, and won him to delight.
O truth and pain immortally bound together!
O lamp the storm made bright!

Still on those heights prophetic winds are raving,
Heath and harebell intone a plainsong grief:
'Shrink, soul of man, shrink into your valleys –
Too sharp that agony, that spring too brief!
Love, though your love is but the forged engraving
Of hope on a stricken leaf!'

Is there one whom blizzards warm and rains enkindle
And the bitterest furnace could no more refine?
Anywhere one too proud for consolation,
Burning for pure freedom so that he will pine,
Yes, to the grave without her? Let him mingle
His barren dust with mine.

But is there one who faithfully has planted
His seed of light in the heart's deepest scar?
When the night is darkest, when the wind is keenest,
He, he shall find upclimbing from afar
Over his pain my chaste, my disenchanted
And death-rebuking star.

BIRTHDAY POEM FOR THOMAS HARDY

Is it birthday weather for you, dear soul?
Is it fine your way,
With tall moon-daisies alight, and the mole
Busy, and elegant hares at play
By meadow paths where once you would stroll
In the flush of day?

I fancy the beasts and flowers there beguiled
By a visitation
That casts no shadow, a friend whose mild
Inquisitive glance lights with compassion,
Beyond the tomb, on all of this wild
And humbled creation.

It's hard to believe a spirit could die
Of such generous glow,
Or to doubt that somewhere a bird-sharp eye
Still broods on the capers of men below,

A stern voice asks the Immortals why
They should plague us so.

Dear poet, wherever you are, I greet you.
Much irony, wrong,
Innocence you'd find here to tease or entreat you,
And many the fate-fires have tempered strong,
But none that in ripeness of soul could meet you
Or magic of song.

Great brow, frail frame – gone. Yet you abide
In the shadow and sheen,
All the mellowing traits of a countryside
That nursed your tragi-comical scene;
And in us, warmer-hearted and brisker-eyed
Since you have been.

THE CHRISTMAS TREE

Put out the lights now!
Look at the Tree, the rough tree dazzled
In oriole plumes of flame,
Tinselled with twinkling frost fire, tasselled
With stars and moons – the same
That yesterday hid in the spinney and had no fame
'Till we put out the lights now.

Hard are the nights now:
The fields at moonrise turn to agate,
Shadows are cold as jet;
In dyke and furrow, in copse and faggot
The frost's tooth is set;
And stars are the sparks whirled out by the north wind's
        fret
On the flinty nights now.

So feast your eyes now
On mimic star and moon-cold bauble:
Worlds may wither unseen,
But the Christmas Tree is a tree of fable,
A phoenix in evergreen,
And the world cannot change or chill what its mysteries
        mean
To your hearts and eyes now.

The vision dies now
Candle by candle: the tree that embraced it
Returns to its own kind,
To be earthed again and weather as best it
May the frost and the wind.
Children, it too had its hour – you will not mind
If it lives or dies now.

II

Two Narrative Poems

FLIGHT TO AUSTRALIA

Sing we the two lieutenants, Parer and M'Intosh,
After the War wishing to hie them home to Australia,
Planned they would take a high way, a hazardous crazy
    air-way:
Death their foregone conclusion, a flight headlong to
    failure,
We said. For no silver posh
Plane was their pigeon, no dandy dancer quick-stepping
    through heaven,
But a craft of obsolete design, a condemned D.H. nine;
Sold for a song it was, patched up though to write an
    heroic
Line across the world as it reeled on its obstinate stoic
Course to that southern haven.

On January 8, 1920, their curveting wheels kissed
England goodbye. Over Hounslow huddled in morning
    mist
They rose and circled like buzzards while we rubbed our
    sleepy eyes:
Like a bird scarce-fledged they flew, whose flying hours
    are few –
Still dear is the nest but deeper its desire unto the skies –
And they left us to our sleeping.

They felt earth's warning tug on their wings: vain to
    advance
Asking a thoroughfare through the angers of the air
On so flimsy a frame: but they pulled up her nose and
    the earth went sloping
Away, and they aimed for France.

Fog first, a wet blanket, a kill-joy, the primrose-of-
    morning's blight,
Blotting out the dimpled sea, the ample welcome of land,
The gay glance from the bright
Cliff-face behind, snaring the sky with treachery, sneering
At hope's loss of height. But they charged it, flying
    blind;
They took a compass-bearing against that dealer of
    doubt,
As a saint when the field of vision is fogged gloriously
    steels
His spirit against the tainter of air, the elusive taunter:
They climbed to win a way out,
Then downward dared till the moody waves snarled at
    their wheels.

Landing at last near Conteville, who had skimmed the
    crest of oblivion,
They could not rest, but rose and flew on to Paris, and
    there

Trivially were delayed – a defective petrol feed –
Three days: a time hung heavy on
Hand and heart, till they leapt again to the upper air,
Their element, their lover, their angel antagonist.
Would have taken a fall without fame, but the sinewy
     framework the wrist
Of steel the panting engine wrestled well: and they went
South while the going was good, as a swallow that guide
     nor goad
Needs on his sunny scent.

At Lyons the petrol pump failed again, and forty-eight
     hours
They chafed to be off, the haughty champions whose
     breathing-space
Was an horizon span and the four winds their fan.
Over Italy's shores
A reverse, the oil ran out and cursing they turned about
Losing a hundred miles to find a landing-place.
Not a coast for a castaway this, no even chance of
     alighting
On sward or wind-smooth sand:
A hundred miles without pressure they flew, the engine
     fighting
For breath, and its heart nearly burst before they
     dropped to land.

And now the earth they had spurned rose up against
     them in anger,

Tier upon tier it towered, the terrible Apennines:
No sanctuary there for wings, not flares nor landing-
      lines,
No hope of floor and hangar.
Yet those ice-tipped spears that disputed the passage
      set spurs
To their two hundred and forty horse power; grimly
      they gained
Altitude, though the hand of heaven was heavy upon
      them,
The downdraught from the mountains: though des-
      perate eddies spun them
Like a coin, yet unkindly tossed their luck came upper-
      most
And mastery remained.

Air was all ambushes round them, was avalanche earth-
      quake
Quicksand, a funnel deep as doom, till climbing steep
They crawled like a fly up the face of perpendicular
      night
And levelled, finding a break
At fourteen thousand feet. Here earth is shorn from
      sight:
Deadweight a darkness hangs on their eyelids, and they
      bruise
Their eyes against a void: vindictive the cold airs close

Down like a trap of steel and numb them from head to
    heel;
Yet they kept an even keel,
For their spirit reached forward and took the controls
    while their fingers froze.

They had not heard the last of death. When the moun-
    tains were passed,
He raised another crest, the long crescendo of pain
Kindled to climax, the plane
Took fire. Alone in the sky with the breath of their
    enemy
Hot in their face they fought: from three thousand feet
    they tilted
Over, side-slipped away – a trick for an ace, a race
And running duel with death: flame streamed out
    behind,
A crimson scarf of, as life-blood out of a wound, but the
    wind
Of their downfall staunched it; death wilted,
Lagged and died out in smoke – he could not stay their
    pace.

A lull for a while. The powers of hell rallied their
    legions.
On Parer now fell the stress of the flight; for the plane
    had been bumped,
Buffeted, thrashed by the air almost beyond repair:

But he tinkered and coaxed, and they limped
Over the Adriatic on into warmer regions.
Erratic their course to Athens, to Crete: coolly they
    rode her
Like a tired horse at the water-jumps, they jockeyed
    her over seas,
Till they came at last to a land whose dynasties of sand
Had seen Alexander, Napoleon, many a straddling in-
    vader,
But never none like these.

England to Cairo, a joy-ride, a forty-hour journey at
    most,
Had cost them forty-four days. What centuried strata
    of life
Fuelled the fire that haled them to heaven, the power
    that held them
Aloft? For their plane was a laugh,
A patch, brittle as matchstick, a bubble, a lift for a
    ghost:
Bolts always working loose of propeller, cylinder, bearer;
Instruments faulty; filter, magneto, each strut unsound.
Yet after four days, though we swore she never could
    leave the ground,
We saw her in headstrong haste diminish towards the
    east —
That makeshift, mad sky-farer.

Aimed they now for Baghdad, unwritten in air's annals
A voyage. But theirs the fate all flights of logic to re-
    fute,
Who obeyed no average law, who buoyed the viewless
    channels
Of sky with a courage steadfast, luminous. Safe they
    crossed
Sinai's desert, and daring
The Nejd, the unneighbourly waste of Arabia, yet
    higher soaring
(Final a fall there for birds of passage, limed and lost
In shifty the sand's embrace) all day they strove to
    climb
Through stormy rain: but they felt her shorten her
    stride and falter,
And they fell at evening time.

Slept that night beside their machine, and the next
    morning
Raider Arabs appeared reckoning this stranded bird
A gift: like cobras they struck, and their gliding shadows
    athwart
The sand were all their warning.
But the aeronauts, knowing iron the coinage here, had
    brought
Mills bombs and revolvers, and M'Intosh held them off
While Parer fought for life –

A spark, the mechanic's right answer, and finally
     wrought
A miracle, for the dumb engine spoke and they rose
Convulsively out of the clutch of the desert, the clench
     of their foes.

Orchestrate this theme, artificer-poet. Imagine
The roll, crackling percussion, quickening tempo of
     engine
For a start: the sound as they soar, an octave-upward
     slur
Scale of sky ascending:
Hours-held note of level flight, a beat unhurried,
Sustaining undertone of movement never-ending:
Wind shrill on the ailerons, flutes and fifes in a flurry
Devilish when they dive, plucking of tense stays.
These hardly heard it, who were the voice, the heavenly
     air
That sings above always.

We have seen the extremes, the burning, the freezing,
     the outward face
Of their exploit; heroic peaks, tumbling-to-zero de-
     pressions:
Little our graph can show, the line they traced through
     space,
Of the heart's passionate patience.

How soft drifts of sleep piled on their senses deep
And they dug themselves out often: how the plane was
    a weight that hung
And swung on their aching nerve; how din drilled
    through the skull
And sight sickened – so slow earth filtered past below.
Yet nerve failed never, heart clung
To height, and the brain kept its course and the hand
    its skill.

Baghdad renewed a propeller damaged in desert. Arid
Baluchistan spared them that brought down and spoilt
    with thirst
Armies of Alexander. To Karachi they were carried
On cloud-back: fragile as tinder their plane, but the
    winds were tender
Now to their need, and nursed
Them along till teeming India made room for them to
    alight
Wilting her wings, the sweltering suns had moulted her
    bright
Plumage, rotten with rain
The fabric: but they packed her with iron washers and
    tacked her
Together, good for an hour, and took the air again.

Feats for a hundred flights, they were prodigal of: a
    fairest
CDL—C

Now to tell – how they foiled death when the engine
    failed
Above the Irrawaddy, over close-woven forest.
What shoals for a pilot there, what a snarled passage
    and dark
Shelves down to doom and grip
Of green! But look, balanced superbly, quick off the
    mark
Swooping like centre three-quarter whose impetus
    storms a gap –
Defenders routed, rooted their feet, and their arms are
    mown
Aside, that high or low aim at his overthrow –
M'Intosh touched her down.

And they picked her up out of it somehow and put her
    at the air, a
Sorry hack for such steeplechasing, to leap the sky.
'We'll fly this bloody crate till it falls to bits at our feet,'
Said the mechanic Parer.
And at Moulmein soon they crashed; and the plane by
    their spirit's high
Tension long pinned, girded and guarded from
    dissolution,
Fell to bits at their feet. Wrecked was the undercarriage,
Radiator cracked, in pieces, compasses crocked;
Fallen all to confusion.

Their winged hope was a heap of scrap, but unsplintered
    their courage.

Six weeks they worked in sun-glare and jungle damps,
    assembling
Fragments to make airworthy what was worth not its
    weight in air.
As a surgeon, grafter of skin, as a setter of bones tumb-
    ling
Apart, they had power to repair
This good for naught but the grave: they livened her
    engine and gave
Fuselage faith to rise rejuvenated from ruin.
Went with them stowaways, not knowing what hazard
    they flew in –
Bear-cubs, a baby alligator, lizards and snakes galore;
Mascots maybe, for the plane though twice she was
    floored again
Always came up for more.

Till they came to the pitiless mountains of Timor. Yet
    these, untamed,
Not timorous, against the gradient and Niagara of air
    they climbed
Scarce-skimming the summits; and over the shark-
    toothed Timor sea

Lost their bearings, but shirked not the odds, the deaths
　　that lurked
A million to one on their trail:
They reached out to the horizon and plucked their des-
　　tiny.
On for eight hours they flew blindfold against the un-
　　known,
And the oil began to fail
And their flying spirit waned – one pint of petrol re-
　　mained
When the land stood up to meet them and they came
　　into their own.

Southward still to Melbourne, the bourn of their flight,
　　they pressed
Till at last near Culcairn, like a last fretted leaf
Falling from brave autumn into earth's breast,
D.H. nine, their friend that had seen them to the end,
Gave up her airy life.
The Southern Cross was splendid above the spot where
　　she fell,
The end of her rainbow curve over our weeping day:
And the flyers, glad to be home, unharmed by that
　　dizzy fall,
Dazed as the dead awoken from death, stepped out of
　　the broken
Body and went away.

THE NABARA

*'They preferred, because of the rudeness of their heart,
to die rather than to surrender.'*

PHASE ONE

FREEDOM is more than a word, more than the base
    coinage
Of statesmen, the tyrant's dishonoured cheque, or the
    dreamer's mad
Inflated currency. She is mortal, we know, and made
In the image of simple men who have no taste for
    carnage
But sooner kill and are killed than see that image be-
    trayed.
Mortal she is, yet rising always refreshed from her ashes:
She is bound to earth, yet she flies as high as a passage
    bird
To home wherever man's heart with seasonal warmth is
    stirred:
Innocent is her touch as the dawn's, but still it unleashes
The ravisher shades of envy. Freedom is more than a
    word.

I see man's heart two-edged, keen both for death and
    creation.

As a sculptor rejoices, stabbing and mutilating the stone
Into a shapelier life, and the two joys make one –
So man is wrought in his hour of agony and elation
To efface the flesh to reveal the crying need of his bone.
Burning the issue was beyond their mild forecasting
For those I tell of – men used to the tolerable joy and
      hurt
Of simple lives: they coveted never an epic part;
But history's hand was upon them and hewed an ever-
      lasting
Image of freedom out of their rude and stubborn heart.

The year, Nineteen-thirty-seven: month, March: the
      men, descendants
Of those Iberian fathers, the inquiring ones who would
      go
Wherever the sea-ways led: a pacific people, slow
To feel ambition, loving their laws and their indepen-
      dence –
Men of the Basque country, the Mar Cantábrico.
Fishermen, with no guile outside their craft, they had
      weathered
Often the sierra-ranked Biscayan surges, the wet
Fog of the Newfoundland Banks: they were fond of
      pelota: they met
No game beyond their skill as they swept the sea to-
      gether,
Until the morning they found the leviathan in their net.

Government trawlers *Nabara, Guipuzkoa, Bizkaya,*
Donostia, escorting across blockaded seas
Galdames with her cargo of nickel and refugees
From Bayonne to Bilbao, while the crest of war curled
    higher
Inland over the glacial valleys, the ancient ease.
On the morning of March the fifth, a chill North-
    Wester fanned them,
Fogging the glassy waves: what uncharted doom lay low
There in the fog athwart their course, they could not
    know:
Stout were the armed trawlers, redoubtable those who
    manned them –
Men of the Basque country, the Mar Cantábrico.

Slowly they nosed ahead, while under the chill North-
    Wester
Nervous the sea crawled and twitched like the skin of a
    beast
That dreams of the chase, the kill, the blood-beslavered
    feast:
They too, the light-hearted sailors, dreamed of a fine
    fiesta,
Flags and their children waving, when they won home
    from the east.
Vague as images seen in a misted glass or the vision
Of crystal-gazer, the ships huddled, receded, neared,

Threading the weird fog-maze that coiled their funnels
    and bleared
Day's eye. They were glad of the fog till *Galdames* lost
    position
– Their convoy, precious in life and metal – and dis-
    appeared.

But still they held their course, the confident ear-ringed
    captains,
Unerring towards the landfall, nor guessed how the
    land lay,
How the guardian fog was a guide to lead them all
    astray.
For now, at a wink, the mist rolled up like the film that
    curtains
A saurian's eye; and into the glare of an evil day
Bizkaya, *Guipuzkoa*, *Nabara*, and the little
Donostia stepped at intervals; and sighted, alas,
Blocking the sea and sky a mountain they might not
    pass,
An isle thrown up volcanic and smoking, a giant in
    metal
Astride their path – the rebel cruiser, *Canarias*.

A ship of ten thousand tons she was, a heavyweight
    fighter
To the cocky bantam trawlers: and under her armament
Of eight- and four-inch guns there followed obedient

Towards Pasajes a prize just seized, an Estonian freighter
Laden with arms the exporters of death to Spain had
    sent.
A hush, the first qualm of conflict, falls on the cruiser's
    burnished
Turrets, the trawlers' grimy decks: fiercer the lime-
Light falls, and out of the solemn ring the late mists
    climb,
And ship to ship the antagonists gaze at each other
    astonished
Across the quaking gulf of the sea for a moment's time.

The trawlers' men had no chance or wish to elude the
    fated
Encounter. Freedom to these was natural pride that
    runs
Hot as the blood, their climate and heritage, dearer
    than sons.
Bizkaya, *Guipuzkoa*, knowing themselves outweighted,
Drew closer to draw first blood with their pairs of four-
    inch guns.
Aboard *Canarias* the German gun-layers stationed
Brisk at their intricate batteries – guns and men both
    trained
To a hair in accuracy, aimed at a pitiless end –
Fired, and the smoke rolled forth over the unimpassioned
Face of a day where nothing certain but death remained.

PHASE TWO

The sound of the first salvo skimmed the ocean and
    thumped
Cape Machichaco's granite ribs: it rebounded where
The salt-sprayed trees grow tough from wrestling the
    wind: it jumped
From isle to rocky isle: it was heard by women while
They walked to shrine or market, a warning they must
    fear.
But, beyond their alarm, as
Though that sound were also a signal for fate to strip
Luck's last green shoot from the falling stock of the
    Basques, *Galdames*
Emerged out of the mist that lingered to the west
Under the reeking muzzles of the rebel battleship:

Which instantly threw five shells over her funnel, and
    threw
Her hundred women and children into a slaughter-yard
    panic
On the deck they imagined smoking with worse than
    the foggy dew,
So that *Galdames* rolled as they slipped, clawed,
    trampled, reeled
Away from the gape of the cruiser's guns. A spasm
    galvanic,

Fear's chemistry, shocked the women's bodies, a moment before
Huddled like sheep in a mist, inert as bales of rag,
A mere deck-cargo: but more
Than furies now, for they stormed *Galdames'* bridge and swarmed
Over her captain and forced him to run up the white flag.

Signalling the Estonian, 'Heave-to', *Canarias* steamed
Leisurely over to make sure of this other prize:
Over-leisurely was her reckoning – she never dreamed
The Estonian in that pause could be snatched from her shark-shape jaws
By ships of minnow size.
Meanwhile *Nabara* and *Guipuzkoa*, not reluctant
For closer grips while their guns and crews were still entire,
Thrust forward: twice *Guipuzkoa* with a deadly jolt was rocked, and
The sea spat up in geysers of boiling foam, as the cruiser's
Heavier guns boxed them in a torrid zone of fire.

And now the little *Donostia* who lay with her 75's
Dumb in the offing – her weapons against that leviathan
Impotent as pen-knives –

Witnessed a bold manoeuvre, a move of genius, never
In naval history told. She saw *Bizkaya* run
Ahead of her consorts, a berserk atom of steel, audacious,
Her signal-flags soon to flutter like banderillas, straight
Towards the Estonian speeding, a young bull over the
    spacious
And foam-distraught arena, till the sides of the freight-
    ship screen her
From *Canarias* that will see the point of her charge too
    late.

'Who are you and where are you going?' the flags of
    Bizkaya questioned.
'Carrying arms and forced to go to Pasajes,' replied
The Estonian. 'Follow me to harbour.' 'Cannot, am
    threatened.'
Bizkaya's last word – 'Turn at once!' – and she points
    her peremptory guns
Against the freighter's mountainous flanks that blankly
    hide
This fluttering language and flaunt of signal insolence
From the eyes of *Canarias*. At last the rebels can see
That the two ships' talk meant a practical joke at their
    expense:
They see the Estonian veering away, to Bermeo steer-
    ing,
Bizkaya under her lee.

(To the Basques that ship was a tonic, for she carried
    some million rounds
Of ammunition: to hearts grown sick with hope deferred
And the drain of their country's wounds
She brought what most they needed in face of the aid
    evaded
And the cold delay of those to whom freedom was only
    a word.)*
Owlish upon the water sat the *Canarias*
Mobbed by those darting trawlers, and her signals
    blinked in vain
After the freighter, that still she believed too large to
    pass
Into Bermeo's port – a prize she fondly thought,
When she'd blown the trawlers out of the water, she'd
    take again.

Brisk at their intricate batteries the German gun-layers
    go
About death's business, knowing their longer reach must
    foil

*Cf. Byron's comments upon 'Non-Intervention' in *The Age of Bronze:*
    Lone, lost, abandoned in their utmost need
    By Christians, unto whom they gave their creed,
    The desolated lands, the ravaged isle,
    The fostered feud encouraged to beguile,
    The aid evaded, and the cold delay
    Prolonged but in the hope to make a prey:
    These, these shall tell the tale, and Greece can show
    The false friend worse than the infuriate foe.

The impetus, break the heart of the government ships: each blow
Deliberately they aim, and tiger-striped with flame
Is the jungle mirk of the smoke as their guns leap and recoil.
The Newfoundland trawlers feel
A hail and hurricane the like they have never known
In all their deep-sea life: they wince at the squalls of steel
That burst on their open decks, rake them and leave them wrecks,
But still they fight on long into the sunless afternoon.

– Fought on, four guns against the best of the rebel navy,
Until *Guipuzkoa's* crew could stanch the fires no more
That gushed from her gashes and seeped nearer the magazine. Heavy
At heart they turned away for the Nervion that day:
Their ship, *Guipuzkoa*, wore
Flame's rose on her heart like a decoration of highest honour
As listing she reeled into Las Arenas; and in a row
On her deck there lay, smoke-palled, that oriflamme's crackling banner
Above them, her dead – a quarter of the fishermen who had fought her –
Men of the Basque country, the Mar Cantábrico.

PHASE THREE

And now the gallant *Nabara* was left in the ring alone,
The sky hollow around her, the fawning sea at her side:
But the ear-ringed crew in their berets stood to the
    guns, and cried
A fresh defiance down
The ebb of the afternoon, the battle's darkening tide.
Honour was satisfied long since, they had held and har-
    ried
A ship ten times their size; they well could have called
    it a day.
But they hoped, if a little longer they kept the cruiser
    in play,
Galdames with the wealth of life and metal she carried
Might make her getaway.

Canarias, though easily she outpaced and out-gunned
    her,
Finding this midge could sting
Edged off, and beneath a wedge of smoke steamed in a
    ring
On the rim of the trawler's range, a circular storm of
    thunder.
But always *Nabara* turned her broadside, manoeuvering
To keep both guns on the target, scorning safety devices.
Slower now battle's tempo, irregular the beat
Of gunfire in the heart

Of the afternoon, the distempered sky sank to the crisis,
Shell-shocked the sea tossed and hissed in delirious heat.

The battle's tempo slowed, for the cruiser could take
　　　her time,
And the guns of *Nabara* grew
Red-hot, and of fifty-two Basque seamen had been her
　　　crew
Many were dead already, the rest filthy with grime
And their comrades' blood, weary with wounds all but
　　　a few.
Between two fires they fought, for the sparks that flash-
　　　ing spoke
From the cruiser's thunder-bulk were answered on their
　　　own craft
By traitor flames that crawled out of every cranny and
　　　rift
Blinding them all with smoke.
At half-past four *Nabara* was burning fore and aft.

What buoyancy of will
Was theirs to keep her afloat, no vessel now but a sieve –
So jarred and scarred, the rivets starting, no inch of her
　　　safe
From the guns of the foe that wrapped her in a cyclone
　　　of shrieking steel!
Southward the sheltering havens showed clear, the cliffs
　　　and the surf

Familiar to them from childhood, the shapes of a life
    still dear:
But dearer still to see
Those shores insured for life from the shadow of tyranny.
Freedom was not on their lips; it was what made them
    endure,
A steel spring in the yielding flesh, a thirst to be free.

And now from the little *Donostia* that lay with her 75's
Dumb in the offing, they saw *Nabara* painfully lower
A boat, which crawled like a shattered crab slower and
    slower
Towards them. They cheered the survivors, thankful to
    save these lives
At least. They saw each rower,
As the boat dragged alongside, was wounded – the oars
    they held
Dripping with blood, a bloody skein reeled out in their
    wake:
And they swarmed down the rope-ladders to rescue
    these men so weak
From wounds they must be hauled
Aboard like babies. And then they saw they had made a
    mistake.

For, standing up in the boat,
A man of that grimy boat's-crew hailed them: 'Our
    officer asks
You give us your bandages and all your water-casks,

Then run for Bermeo. We're going to finish this game
  of *pelota*.'
Donostia's captain begged them with tears to escape:
  but the Basques
Would play their game to the end.
They took the bandages, and cursing at his delay
They took the casks that might keep the fires on their
  ship at bay;
And they rowed back to *Nabara*, trailing their blood
  behind
Over the water, the sunset and crimson ebb of their day.

For two hours more they fought, while *Nabara* beneath
  their feet
Was turned to a heap of smouldering scrap-iron. Once
  again
The flames they had checked a while broke out. When
  the forward gun
Was hit, they turned about
Bringing the after gun to bear. They fought in pain
And the instant knowledge of death: but the waters
  filling their riven
Ship could not quench the love that fired them. As each
  man fell
To the deck, his body took fire as if death made visible
That burning spirit. For two more hours they fought,
  and at seven
They fired their last shell.

Of her officers all but one were dead. Of her engineers
All but one were dead. Of the fifty-two that had sailed
In her, all were dead but fourteen – and each of these
     half killed
With wounds. And the night-dew fell in a hush of ashen
     tears,
And *Nabara's* tongue was stilled.
Southward the sheltering havens grew dark, the cliffs
     and the green
Shallows they knew; where their friends had watched
     them as evening wore
To a glowing end, who swore
Nabara must show a white flag now, but saw instead the
     fourteen
Climb into their matchwood boat and fainting pull for
     the shore.

Canarias lowered a launch that swept in a greyhound's
     curve
Pitiless to pursue
And cut them off. But that bloodless and all-but-phan-
     tom crew
Still gave no soft concessions to fate: they strung their
     nerve
For one last fling of defiance, they shipped their oars
     and threw
Hand-grenades at the launch as it circled about to
     board them.

But the strength of the hands that had carved them a
    hold on history
Failed them at last: the grenades fell short of the enemy,
Who grappled and overpowered them,
While *Nabara* sank by the stern in the hushed Cantabrian
    sea.

*

They bore not a charmed life. They went into battle
    foreseeing
Probable loss, and they lost. The tides of Biscay flow
Over the obstinate bones of many, the winds are
    sighing
Round prison walls where the rest are doomed like their
    ship to rust —
Men of the Basque country, the Mar Cantábrico.
Simple men who asked of their life no mythical splen-
    dour,
They loved its familiar ways so well that they preferred
In the rudeness of their heart to die rather than to sur-
    render . . .
Mortal these words and the deed they remember, but
    cast a seed
Shall flower for an age when freedom is man's creative
    word.

Freedom was more than a word, more than the base
    coinage

Of politicians who hiding behind the skirts of peace
They had defiled, gave up that country to rack and
    carnage:
For whom, indelibly stamped with history's contempt,
Remains but to haunt the blackened shell of their
    policies.
For these I have told of, freedom was flesh and blood –
    a mortal
Body, the gun-breech hot to its touch: yet the battle's
    height
Raised it to love's meridian and held it awhile immortal;
And its light through time still flashes like a star's that
    has turned to ashes,
Long after *Nabara's* passion was quenched in the sea's
    heart.

Lyrical and Reflective Poems
1929–36

FOR I HAD BEEN A MODERN MOTH

For I had been a modern moth and hurled
Myself on many a flaming world,
To find its globe was glass.
In you alone
I met the naked light, by you became
Veteran of a flame
That burns away all but the warrior bone.
And I shall know, if time should falsify
This star the company of my night,
Mine is the heron's flight
Which makes a solitude of any sky.

MY LOVE IS A TOWER

My love is a tower.
Standing up in her
I parley with planets
And the casual wind.
Arcturus may grind
Against our wall: he whets

A tropic appetite,
And decorates our night.
'What happier place
For Johnny Head-in-Air,
Who never would hear
Time mumbling at the base?'

I will not hear, for she's
My real Antipodes,
And our ingrowing loves
Shall meet below earth's spine
And there shall intertwine,
Though Babel falls above.
Time, we allow, destroys
All aërial toys:
But to assail love's heart
He has no strategy,
Unless he suck up the sea
And pull the earth apart.

HOW THEY WOULD JEER AT US

How they would jeer at us—
Ulysses, Herodotus,
The hard-headed Phoenicians
Or, of later nations,

Columbus, the Pilgrim Fathers
And a thousand others
Who laboured only to find
Some pittance of new ground,
Merchandise or women.
Those rude and bourgeois seamen
Got glory thrown in
As it were with every ton
Of wave that swept their boat,
And would have preferred a coat
For keeping off the spray.

Since the heroes lie
Entombed with the recipe
Of epic in their heart,
And have buried – it seems – that art
Of minding one's own business
Magnanimously, for us
There's nothing but to recant
Ambition, and be content
Like the poor child at play
To find a holiday
In the sticks and mud
Of a familiar road.

DESIRE IS A WITCH

DESIRE is a witch
And runs against the clock.
It can unstitch
The decent hem
Where space tacks on to time:
It can unlock
Pandora's privacies.

It puffs in these
Top-gallants of the mind,
And away I stand
On the elemental gale
Into an ocean
That the liar Lucian
Had never dared retail.

When my love leans with all
Her shining breast and shoulder,
I know she is older
Than Ararat the hill,
And yet more young
Than the first daffodil
That ever shews a spring.

When her eyes delay
On me, so deep are they
Tunnelled by love, although
You poured Atlantic
In this one and Pacific
In the other, I know
They would not overflow.

Desire clicks back
Like cuckoo into clock;
Leaves me to explain
Eyes that a tear will drown
And a body where youth
Nor age will long remain
To implicate the truth.

It seems that we must call
Anything truth whose well
Is deep enough;
For the essential
Philosopher-stone, desire,
Needs no other proof
Than its own fire.

WHEN NATURE PLAYS

WHEN nature plays hedge-schoolmaster,
Shakes out the gaudy map of summer
And shows me charabanc, rose, barley-ear
And every bright-winged hummer,

He only would require of me
To be the sponge of natural laws
And learn no more of that cosmography
Than passes through the pores.

Why must I then unleash my brain
To sweat after some revelation
Behind the rose, heedless if truth maintain
On the rose-bloom her station?

When bullying April bruised mine eyes
With sleet-bound appetites and crude
Experiments of green, I still was wise
And kissed the blossoming rod.

Now summer brings what April took,
Riding with fanfares from the south,
And I should be no Solomon to look
My Sheba in the mouth.

Charabancs shout along the lane
And summer gales bay in the wood
No less superbly because I can't explain
What I have understood.

Let logic analyse the hive,
Wisdom's content to have the honey:
So I'll go bite the crust of things and thrive
While hedgerows still are sunny.

WITH ME, MY LOVER MAKES

WITH me, my lover makes
    The clock assert its chime:
But when she goes, she takes
    The mainspring out of time.

Yet this time-wrecking charm
    Were better than love dead
And its hollow alarum
    Hammered out on lead.

Why should I fear that Time
    Will superannuate
These workmen of my rhyme –
    Love, despair and hate?

Fleeing the herd, I came
　To a graveyard on a hill,
And felt its mould proclaim
　The bone gregarious still.

Boredoms and agonies
　Work out the rhythm of bone:
No peace till creature his
　Creator has outgrown.

Passion dies from the heart
　But to infect the marrow;
Holds dream and act apart
　Till the man discard his narrow

Sapience and folly
　Here, where the graves slumber
In a green melancholy
　Of overblown summer.

THOSE HIMALAYAS OF THE MIND

THOSE Himalayas of the mind
Are not so easily possessed;
There's more than precipice and storm
Between you and your Everest.

You who declare the peak of peaks
Alone will satisfy your want,
Can you distil a grain of snow?
Can you digest an adamant?

Better by far the household cock
Scratching the common yard for corn,
Whose rainy voice all night at will
Can signify a private dawn.

Another bird, sagacious too,
Circles in plain bewilderment
Where shoulder to shoulder long waves march
Towards a magnetic continent.

'What are these rocks impede our pomp?'
Gesticulating to the sun
The waves part ranks, sidle and fume,
Then close behind them and march on.

The waves advance, the Absolute Cliffs
Unaccountably repel:
They linger grovelling; where assault
Has failed, attrition may tell.

The bird sees nothing to the point;
Shrugs an indifferent wing; proceeds
From rock to rock in the mid-ocean
Peering for barnacles and weeds.

CDL—D

THE HAWK COMES DOWN
FROM THE AIR

THE hawk comes down from the air.
Sharpening his eye upon
A wheeling horizon
Turned scrutiny to prayer.

He guessed the prey that cowers
Below, and learnt to keep
The distance which can strip
Earth to its blank contours.

Then trod the air, content
With contemplation till
The truth of valley and hill
Should be self-evident.

Or as the little lark
Who veins the sky with song,
Asking from dawn to dark
No revenues of spring:

But with the night descends
Into his chosen tree,
And the famed singer ends
In anonymity.

So from a summer's height
I come into my peace;
The wings have earned their night,
And the song may cease.

SUPPOSE THAT WE...

Suppose that we, to-morrow or the next day,
Came to an end – in storm the shafting broken,
Or a mistaken signal, the flange lifting –
Would that be premature, a text for sorrow?

Say what endurance gives or death denies us.
Love's proved in its creation, not eternity:
Like leaf or linnet the true heart's affection
Is born, dies later, asks no reassurance.

Over dark wood rises one dawn felicitous,
Bright through awakened shadows fall her crystal
Cadenzas, and once for all the wood is quickened.
So our joys visit us, and it suffices.

Nor fear we now to live who in the valley
Of the shadow of life have found a causeway;
For love restores the nerve and love is under
Our feet resilient. Shall we be weary?

Some say we walk out of Time altogether
This way into a region where the primrose
Shows an immortal dew, sun at meridian
Stands up for ever and in scent the lime tree.

This is land which later we may tell of.
Here-now we know, what death cannot diminish
Needs no replenishing; yet certain are, though
Dying were well enough, to live is better.

Passion has grown full man by his first birthday.
Running across the bean-fields in a south wind,
Fording the river mouth to feel the tide-race –
Child's play that was, though proof of our possessions.

Now our research is done, measured the shadow,
The plains mapped out, the hills a natural boundary.
Such and such is our country. There remains to
Plough up the meadowland, reclaim the marshes.

BEAUTY'S END IS IN SIGHT

BEAUTY's end is in sight,
Terminus where all feather joys alight.
Wings that flew lightly
Fold and are iron. We see
The thin end of mortality.

We must a little part,
And sprouting seed crack our cemented heart.
Who would get an heir
Initial loss must bear:
A part of each will be elsewhere.

What life may now decide
Is past the clutch of caution, the range of pride.
Speaking from the snow
The crocus lets me know
That there is life to come, and go.

NOW SHE IS LIKE THE
WHITE TREE-ROSE

Now she is like the white tree-rose
That takes a blessing from the sun:
Summer has filled her veins with light,
And her warm heart is washed with noon.

Or as a poplar, ceaselessly
Gives a soft answer to the wind:
Cool on the light her leaves lie sleeping,
Folding a column of sweet sound.

Powder the stars. Forbid the night
To wear those brilliants for a brooch.
So soon, dark death, you may close down
The mines that made this beauty rich.

Her thoughts are pleiads, stooping low
O'er glades where nightingale has flown:
And like the luminous night around her
She has at heart a certain dawn.

REST FROM LOVING

REST from loving and be living.
Fallen is fallen past retrieving
The unique flyer dawn's dove
Arrowing down feathered with fire.

Cease denying, begin knowing.
Comes peace this way here comes renewing
With dower of bird and bud knocks
Loud on winter wall on death's door.

Here's no meaning but of morning.
Naught soon of night but stars remaining,
Sink lower, fade, as dark womb
Recedes creation will step clear.

WANING IS NOW THE SENSUAL EYE

WANING is now the sensual eye
Allowed no flaw upon the skin
And burnt away wrinkle and feature,
Fed with pure spirit from within.

Nesciently that vision works.
Just so the pure night-eye, the moon,
Labours, a monumental mason,
To gloss over a world of stone.

Look how she marbled heath and terrace,
Effacing boundary and date.
She took the sky; earth was below her
A shining shell, a featherweight.

No more may pupil love bend over
A plane theorem, black and white.
The interlocking hours revolve,
The globe goes lumbering into light.

Admiral earth breaks out his colours
Bright at the forepeak of the day;
Hills in their hosts escort the sun
And valleys welcome him their way.

Shadow takes depth and shape turns solid:
Far-ranging, the creative eye
Sees arable, marsh, enclosed and common,
Assents to multiplicity.

AS ONE WHO WANDERS...

As one who wanders into old workings
Dazed by the noonday, desiring coolness,
Has found retreat barred by fall of rockface;
Gropes through galleries where granite bruises
Taut palm and panic patters close at heel;
Must move forward as tide to the moon's nod,
As mouth to breast in blindness is beckoned.
Nightmare nags at his elbow and narrows
Horizon to pinpoint, hope to hand's breadth.
Slow drip the seconds, time is stalactite,
For nothing intrudes here to tell the time,
Sun marches not, nor moon with muffled step.
He wants an opening, – only to break out,
To see the dark glass cut by day's diamond,
To relax again in the lap of light.

But we seek a new world through old workings,
Whose hope lies like seed in the loins of earth,
Whose dawn draws gold from the roots of darkness.

Not shy of light nor shrinking from shadow
Like Jesuits in jungle we journey
Deliberately bearing to brutish tribes
Christ's assurance, arts of agriculture.
As a train that travels underground track
Feels current flashed from far-off dynamos,
Our wheels whirling with impetus elsewhere
Generated we run, are ruled by rails.
Train shall spring from tunnel to terminus,
Out on to plain shall the pioneer plunge,
Earth reveal what veins fed, what hill covered.
Lovely the leap, explosion into light.

NOW THE FULL-THROATED
DAFFODILS

Now the full-throated daffodils,
Our trumpeters in gold,
Call resurrection from the ground
And bid the year be bold.

To-day the almond tree turns pink,
The first flush of the spring;
Winds loll and gossip through the town
Her secret whispering

Now too the bird must try his voice
Upon the morning air;
Down drowsy avenues he cries
A novel great affair.

He tells of royalty to be;
How with her train of rose
Summer to coronation comes
Through waving wild hedgerows.

To-day crowds quicken in a street,
The fish leaps in the flood:
Look there, gasometer rises,
And here bough swells to bud.

For our love's luck, our stowaway,
Stretches in his cabin;
Our youngster joy barely conceived
Shows up beneath the skin.

Our joy was but a gusty thing
Without sinew or wit,
An infant flyaway; but now
We make a man of it.

DO NOT EXPECT AGAIN
A PHOENIX HOUR

Do not expect again a phoenix hour,
The triple-towered sky, the dove complaining,
Sudden the rain of gold and heart's first ease
Tranced under trees by the eldritch light of sundown.

By a blazed trail our joy will be returning:
One burning hour throws light a thousand ways,
And hot blood stays into familiar gestures.
The best years wait, the body's plenitude.

Consider then, my lover, this is the end
Of the lark's ascending, the hawk's unearthly hover:
Spring season is over soon and first heatwave;
Grave-browed with cloud ponders the huge horizon.

Draw up the dew. Swell with pacific violence.
Take shape in silence. Grow as the clouds grew.
Beautiful brood the cornlands, and you are heavy;
Leafy the boughs – they also hide big fruit.

BEAUTY BREAKS GROUND...

BEAUTY breaks ground, oh, in strange places.
Seen after cloudburst down the bone-dry watercourses,
In Texas a great gusher, a grain-
Elevator in the Ukraine plain;
To a new generation turns new faces.

Here too fountains will soon be flowing.
Empty the hills where love was lying late, was playing,
Shall spring to life: we shall find there
Milk and honey for love's heir,
Shadow from sun also, deep ground for growing.

My love is a good land. The stranger
Entering here was sure he need prospect no further.
Acres that were the eyes' delight
Now feed another appetite.
What formed her first for seed, for crop must change her.

This is my land. I've overheard it
Making a promise out of clay. All is recorded –
Early green, drought, ripeness, rainfall,
Our village fears and festivals,
When the first tractor came and how we cheered it.

And as the wind whose note will deepen
In the upgrowing tree, who runs for miles to open
His throat above the wood, my song
With that increasing life grew strong,
And will have there a finished form to sleep in.

NOW TO BE WITH YOU...

Now to be with you, elate, unshared,
My kestrel joy, O hoverer in wind,
Over the quarry furiously at rest
Chaired on shoulders of shouting wind.

Where's that unique one, wind and wing married,
Aloft in contact of earth and ether;
Feathery my comet, oh too often
From heaven harried by carrion cares.

No searcher may hope to flush that fleet one
Not to be found by gun or glass,
In old habits, last year's hunting-ground,
Whose beat is wind-wide, whose perch a split second.

But surely will meet him, late or soon,
Who turns a corner into new territory;
Spirit mating afresh shall discern him
On the world's noon-top purely poised.

Void are the valleys, in town no trace,
And dumb the sky-dividing hills:
Swift outrider of lumbering earth
Oh hasten hither my kestrel joy!

BUT TWO THERE ARE...

But Two there are, shadow us everywhere
And will not let us be till we are dead,
Hardening the bones, keeping the spirit spare,
Original in water, earth and air,
Our bitter cordial, our daily bread.

Turning over old follies in ante-room:
For first-born waiting or for late reprieve,
Watching the safety-valve, the slackening loom,
Abed, abroad, at every turn and tomb
A shadow starts, a hand is on your sleeve.

O you, my comrade, now or to-morrow flayed
Alive, crazed by the nibbling nerve; my friend
Whom hate has cornered or whom love betrayed,
By hunger sapped, trapped by a stealthy tide,
Brave for so long but whimpering in the end:

Such are the temporal princes, fear and pain,
Whose borders march with the ice-fields of death,
And from that servitude escape there's none
Till in the grave we set up house alone
And buy our liberty with our last breath.

LET US BE OFF!

LET us be off! Our steam
Is deafening the dome.
The needle in the gauge
Points to a long-banked rage,
And trembles there to show
What a pressure's below.
Valve cannot vent the strain
Nor iron ribs refrain
That furnace in the heart.
Come on, make haste and start
Coupling-rod and wheel
Welded of patient steel,
Piston that will not stir
Beyond the cylinder
To take in its stride
A teeming countryside.

A countryside that gleams
In the sun's weeping beams;
Where wind-pump, byre and barrow
Are mellowed to mild sorrow,
Agony and sweat
Grown over with regret.
What golden vesper hours
Halo the old grey towers,
What honeyed bells in valleys
Embalm our faiths and follies!
Here are young daffodils
Wind-wanton, and the hills
Have made their peace with heaven.
Oh lovely the heart's haven,
Meadows of endless May,
A spirit's holiday!

Traveller, take care,
Pick no flowers there!

NEARING AGAIN THE
LEGENDARY ISLE

Nearing again the legendary isle
Where sirens sang and mariners were skinned,
We wonder now what was there to beguile
That such stout fellows left their bones behind.

Those chorus-girls are surely past their prime,
Voices grow shrill and paint is wearing thin,
Lips that sealed up the sense from gnawing time
Now beg the favour with a graveyard grin.

We have no flesh to spare and they can't bite,
Hunger and sweat have stripped us to the bone;
A skeleton crew we toil upon the tide
And mock the theme-song meant to lure us on:

No need to stop the ears, avert the eyes
From purple rhetoric of evening skies.

LIVE YOU BY LOVE CONFINED

Live you by love confined,
There is no nearer nearness;
Break not his light bounds,
The stars' and seas' harness:
There is nothing beyond,
We have found the land's end.
We'll take no mortal wound
Who felt him in the furnace,
Drowned in his fierceness,
By his midsummer browned:

Nor ever lose awareness
Of nearness and farness
Who've stood at earth's heart careless
Of suns and storms around,
Who have leant on the hedge of the wind,
On the last ledge of darkness.

We are where love has come
To live: he is that river
Which flows and is the same;
He is not the famous deceiver
Nor early-flowering dream.
Content you. Be at home
In me. There's but one room
Of all the house you may never
Share, deny or enter.
There, as a candle's beam
Stands firm and will not waver
Spire-straight in a close chamber,
As though in shadowy cave a
Stalagmite of flame,
The integral spirit climbs
The dark in light for ever.

GOD IS A PROPOSITION

GOD is a proposition,
And we that prove him are his priests, his chosen.
From bare hypothesis
Of strata and wind, of stars and tides, watch me
Construct his universe,
A working model of my majestic notions,
A sum done in the head.
Last week I measured the light, his little finger;
The rest is a matter of time.

God is an electrician,
And they that worship him must worship him
In ampere and in volt.
Scrap sun and moon, your twilight of false gods:
X is not here or there;
Whose lightning scrawls brief cryptograms on sky,
Easy for us to solve;
Whose motions fit our formulae, whose temple
Is a pure apparatus.

God is a statistician:
Offer him all the data; tell him your dreams.
What is your lucky number?

How do you react to bombs? Have you a rival?
Do you really love your wife?
Get yourself taped. Put soul upon the table:
Switch on the arc-lights; watch
Heart's beat, the secret agents of the blood.
Let every cell be observed.

God is a Good Physician,
Gives fruit for hygiene, crops for calories.
Don't touch that dirty man,
Don't drink from the same cup, sleep in one bed:
You know He would not like it.
Young men, cut out those visions, they're bad for the
    eyes:
I'll show you face to face
Eugenics, Eupeptics and Euthanasia,
The clinic Trinity.

TEMPT ME NO MORE

Tempt me no more; for I
Have known the lightning's hour,
The poet's inward pride,
The certainty of power.

Bayonets are closing round.
I shrink; yet I must wring
A living from despair
And out of steel a song.

Though song, though breath be short,
I'll share not the disgrace
Of those that ran away
Or never left the base.

Comrades, my tongue can speak
No comfortable words,
Calls to a forlorn hope,
Gives work and not rewards.

Oh keep the sickle sharp
And follow still the plough:
Others may reap, though some
See not the winter through.

Father, who endest all,
Pity our broken sleep;
For we lie down with tears
And waken but to weep.

And if our blood alone
Will melt this iron earth,
Take it. It is well spent
Easing a saviour's birth.

THOUGH WINTER'S BARRICADE
DELAYS

THOUGH winter's barricade delays,
Another season's in the air;
We'll sow the spring in our young days,
Found a Virginia everywhere.

Look where the ranks of crocuses
Their rebel colours will display
Coming with quick fire to redress
The balance of a wintry day.

Those daffodils that from the mould
Drawing a sweet breath soon shall flower,
With a year's labour get their gold
To spend it on a sunny hour.

They from earth's centre take their time
And from the sun what love they need:
The proud flower burns away its prime,
Eternity lies in the seed.

Follow the kestrel, south or north;
Strict eye, spontaneous wing can tell
A secret. Where he comes to earth
Is the heart's treasure. Mark it well.

Here he hovers. You're on the scent;
Magnetic mountain is not far,
Across no gulf or continent,
Not where you think but where you are.

Stake out your claim. Go downwards. Bore
Through the tough crust. Oh learn to feel
A way in darkness to good ore.
You are the magnet and the steel.

Out of that dark a new world flowers.
There in the womb, in the rich veins
Are tools, dynamos, bridges, towers,
Your tractors and your travelling-cranes.

IN THESE OUR WINTER DAYS

In these our winter days
Death's iron tongue is glib
Numbing with fear all flesh upon
A fiery-hearted globe.

An age once green is buried,
Numbered the hours of light;
Blood-red across the snow our sun
Still trails his faint retreat.

Spring through death's iron guard
Her million blades shall thrust;
Love that was sleeping, not extinct,
Throw off the nightmare crust.

Eyes, though not ours, shall see
Sky-high a signal flame,
The sun returned to power above
A world, but not the same.

LEARNING TO TALK

S ee this small one, tiptoe on
The green foothills of the years,
Views a younger world than yours;
When you go down, he'll be the tall one.

Dawn's dew is on his tongue –
No word for what's behind the sky,
Naming all that meets the eye,
Pleased with sunlight over a lawn.

Hear his laughter. He can't contain
The exquisite moment overflowing.
Limbs leaping, woodpecker flying
Are for him and not hereafter.

Tongue trips, recovers, triumphs,
Turning all ways to express
What the forward eye can guess –
That time is his and earth young.

We are growing too like trees
To give the rising wind a voice:
Eagles shall build upon our verse,
Our winged seeds are to-morrow's sowing.

Yes, we learn to speak for all
Whose hearts here are not at home,
All who march to a better time
And breed the world for which they burn.

Though we fall once, though we often,
Though we fall to rise not again,
From our horizon sons begin;
When we go down, they will be tall ones.

THE CONFLICT

I SANG as one
Who on a tilting deck sings
To keep men's courage up, though the wave hangs
That shall cut off their sun.

As storm-cocks sing,
Flinging their natural answer in the wind's teeth,
And care not if it is waste of breath
Or birth-carol of spring.

As ocean-flyer clings
To height, to the last drop of spirit driving on
While yet ahead is land to be won
And work for wings.

Singing I was at peace,
Above the clouds, outside the ring:
For sorrow finds a swift release in song
And pride its poise.

Yet living here,
As one between two massing powers I live
Whom neutrality cannot save
Nor occupation cheer.

None such shall be left alive:
The innocent wing is soon shot down,
And private stars fade in the blood-red dawn
Where two worlds strive.

The red advance of life
Contracts pride, calls out the common blood,
Beats song into a single blade,
Makes a depth-charge of grief.

Move then with new desires,
For where we used to build and love
Is no man's land, and only ghosts can live
Between two fires.

IN ME TWO WORLDS

In me two worlds at war
Trample the patient flesh,
This lighted ring of sense where clinch
Heir and ancestor.

This moving point of dust
Where past and future meet
Traces their battle-line and shows
Each thrust and counterthrust.

The armies of the dead
Are trenched within my bones,
My blood's their semaphore, their wings
Are watchers overhead.

Their captains stand at ease
As on familiar ground,
The veteran longings of the heart
Serve them for mercenaries.

Conscious of power and pride
Imperially they move
To pacify an unsettled zone –
The life for which they died.

But see, from vision's height
March down the men to come,
And in my body rebel cells
Look forward to the fight.

The insolence of the dead
Breaks on their solid front:
They tap my nerves for power, my veins
To stain their banners red.

These have the spirit's range,
The measure of the mind:
Out of the dawn their fire comes fast
To conquer and to change.

So heir and ancestor
Pursue the inveterate feud,
Making my senses' darkened fields
A theatre of war.

TWO SONGS

I've heard them lilting at loom and belting,
Lasses lilting before dawn of day:
But now they are silent, not gamesome and gallant –
The flowers of the town are rotting away.

There was laughter and loving in the lanes at evening;
Handsome were the boys then, and girls were gay.
But lost in Flanders by medalled commanders
The lads of the village are vanished away.

Cursed be the promise that takes our men from us –
All will be champion if you choose to obey:
They fight against hunger but still it is stronger –
The prime of our land grows cold as the clay.

The women are weary, once lilted so merry,
Waiting to marry for a year and a day:
From wooing and winning, from owning or earning
The flowers of the town are all turned away.

Come, live with me and be my love,
And we will all the pleasures prove
Of peace and plenty, bed and board,
That chance employment may afford.

I'll handle dainties on the docks
And thou shalt read of summer frocks:
At evening by the sour canals
We'll hope to hear some madrigals.

Care on thy maiden brow shall put
A wreath of wrinkles, and thy foot
Be shod with pain: not silken dress
But toil shall tire thy loveliness.

Hunger shall make thy modest zone
And cheat fond death of all but bone –
If these delights thy mind may move,
Then live with me and be my love.

A PROLOGUE

THIS curve of ploughland, one clean stroke
Defining earth's nature constant to four seasons,
Fixes too for ever her simple relationship
With the sky and all systems imaginable there.

This clean red stroke, like a heart-beat of the earth's
        heart
Felt here under the sunlight's velvet hand,

Draws something simple and perfect as breath – that
    leaves
No more to be said,
And yet implies what wonders beyond, what breathing
    cities,
Pastures broad and untainted prairies of air.

This curve – the naked breasts of woman exalted for
    love,
Cradle both and summit of your superb ambition,
Move not more certainly to that far-flying
Among star-fields above even the wind's excitement,
And exhausted eddying down to peace.

Lover's eye is hawk's eye, on the whole earth
Spread for him seeing only the point of desire.
And then there is the poet's –
His gaze that like the moonlight rests on all
In level contemplation, making roof and ruin
Treachery scorn and death into silver syllables
And out of worn fragments a seamless coat.

These I must have; but more.
To see this ploughland curve as a graph of history,
The unregarded sweat that has made it fertile,
Reading between the furrows a desperate appeal
From all whose share in them was bitter as iron,
Hearing the young corn whisper
The wishes of men who had no other voice.

Only then am I able to know the difficult
Birth of our new seed and bear my part of the harvest.

THE ECSTATIC

Lark, skylark, spilling your rubbed and round
Pebbles of sound in air's still lake,
Whose widening circles fill the noon; yet none
Is known so small beside the sun:

Be strong your fervent soaring, your skyward air!
Tremble there, a nerve of song!
Float up there where voice and wing are one,
A singing star, a note of light!

Buoyed, embayed in heaven's noon-wide reaches –
For soon light's tide will turn – oh stay!
Cease not till day streams to the west, then down
That estuary drop down to peace.